MY
2Nd Grade
JOURNAL

★ Draw and Write ★
★ ★ ★ ★

This book belongs to:

• **Name:** _____

• **Teacher:** _____

Blazing Fields Press

Fill your paper with the breathings of your heart.

- William Wordsworth

We hope you enjoy this journal! We love creating a variety of journals for both adults and kids.

For all our products visit us on Amazon at:

Blazing Fields Press

Or online at:
BlazingFields.com

ISBN-10: 1724572644
ISBN-13: 978-1724572646

Blazing Fields Press

Day _____   **Date** _____

My story for today:

_____

_____

_____

_____

_____

_____

_____

_____

Day _____   **Date** _____

My story for today:

_____

_____

_____

_____

_____

_____

_____

_____

Day _____   **Date** _____

My story for today:

_____

_____

_____

_____

_____

_____

_____

_____

Day _____   **Date** _____

My story for today:

_____

_____

_____

_____

_____

_____

_____

_____

Day _____   **Date** _____

My story for today:

_____

_____

_____

_____

_____

_____

_____

_____

Day _____ **Date** _____

My story for today:

_____

_____

_____

_____

_____

_____

_____

_____

Day _____   **Date** _____

My story for today:

_____

_____

_____

_____

_____

_____

_____

_____

Day _____   **Date** _____

My story for today:

_____

_____

_____

_____

_____

_____

_____

_____

Day _____   **Date** _____

My story for today:

_____

_____

_____

_____

_____

_____

_____

_____

Day _____   **Date** _____

My story for today:

_____

_____

_____

_____

_____

_____

_____

Day _____   **Date** _____

My story for today:

_____

_____

_____

_____

_____

_____

_____

_____

Day _____   **Date** _____

My story for today:

_____

_____

_____

_____

_____

_____

_____

_____

Day _____   **Date** _____

My story for today:

_____

_____

_____

_____

_____

_____

_____

_____

Day _____   **Date** _____

My story for today:

_____

_____

_____

_____

_____

_____

_____

_____

Day _____   **Date** _____

My story for today:

_____

_____

_____

_____

_____

_____

_____

_____

_____

Day _____   **Date** _____

My story for today:

_____

_____

_____

_____

_____

_____

_____

_____

Day _____ **Date** _____

My story for today:

_____

_____

_____

_____

_____

_____

_____

Day _____ **Date** _____

My story for today:

_____

_____

_____

_____

_____

_____

_____

_____

Day _____   **Date** _____

My story for today:

_____

_____

_____

_____

_____

_____

_____

_____

Day _____   **Date** _____

My story for today:

_____

_____

_____

_____

_____

_____

_____

_____

Day _____   **Date** _____

My story for today:

_____

_____

_____

_____

_____

_____

_____

_____

Day _____   **Date** _____

My story for today:

_____

_____

_____

_____

_____

_____

_____

_____

Day _____   **Date** _____

My story for today:

_____

_____

_____

_____

_____

_____

_____

Day _____   **Date** _____

My story for today:

_____

_____

_____

_____

_____

_____

_____

_____

Day _____ **Date** _____

My story for today:

_____

_____

_____

_____

_____

_____

_____

_____

Day _____   **Date** _____

My story for today:

_____

_____

_____

_____

_____

_____

_____

_____

Day _____   **Date** _____

My story for today:

_____

_____

_____

_____

_____

_____

_____

_____

Day _____   **Date** _____

My story for today:

_____

_____

_____

_____

_____

_____

_____

Day _____   **Date** _____

My story for today:

_____

_____

_____

_____

_____

_____

_____

_____

_____

Day _____ **Date** _____

My story for today:

_____

_____

_____

_____

_____

_____

_____

_____

Day _____   **Date** _____

My story for today:

_____

_____

_____

_____

_____

_____

_____

_____

Day _____   **Date** _____

My story for today:

_____

_____

_____

_____

_____

_____

_____

_____

Day _____   **Date** _____

My story for today:

_____

_____

_____

_____

_____

_____

_____

Day _____ **Date** _____

My story for today:

_____

_____

_____

_____

_____

_____

_____

_____

Day _____   **Date** _____

My story for today:

_____
_____
_____
_____
_____
_____
_____
_____

Day _____   **Date** _____

My story for today:

_____

_____

_____

_____

_____

_____

_____

_____

Day _____   **Date** _____

My story for today:

_____

_____

_____

_____

_____

_____

_____

Day _____   **Date** _____

My story for today:

_____

_____

_____

_____

_____

_____

_____

_____

Day _____   **Date** _____

My story for today:

_____

_____

_____

_____

_____

_____

_____

Day _____   **Date** _____

My story for today:

_____

_____

_____

_____

_____

_____

_____

_____

Day _____ **Date** _____

My story for today:

_____

_____

_____

_____

_____

_____

_____

Day _____   **Date** _____

My story for today:

_____

_____

_____

_____

_____

_____

_____

_____

_____

Day _____   **Date** _____

My story for today:

_____

_____

_____

_____

_____

_____

_____

_____

Day _____   **Date** _____

My story for today:

_____

_____

_____

_____

_____

_____

_____

_____

Day _____   **Date** _____

My story for today:

_____

_____

_____

_____

_____

_____

_____

_____

Day _____   **Date** _____

My story for today:

_____

_____

_____

_____

_____

_____

_____

_____

Day _____ **Date** _____

My story for today:

_____

_____

_____

_____

_____

_____

_____

_____

Day _____   **Date** _____

My story for today:

_____

_____

_____

_____

_____

_____

_____

_____

Day _____   **Date** _____

My story for today:

_____

_____

_____

_____

_____

_____

_____

Day _____   **Date** _____

My story for today:

_____

_____

_____

_____

_____

_____

_____

_____

Day _____　　**Date** _____

My story for today:

_____

_____

_____

_____

_____

_____

_____

_____

Day _____   **Date** _____

My story for today:

_____

_____

_____

_____

_____

_____

_____

_____

Day _____   **Date** _____

My story for today:

_____

_____

_____

_____

_____

_____

_____

Day _____   **Date** _____

My story for today:

_____

_____

_____

_____

_____

_____

_____

_____

Day _____ **Date** _____

My story for today:

_____

_____

_____

_____

_____

_____

_____

_____

Day _____   **Date** _____

My story for today:

_____

_____

_____

_____

_____

_____

_____

Day _____   **Date** _____

My story for today:

_____

_____

_____

_____

_____

_____

_____

_____

Day _____   **Date** _____

My story for today:

_____

_____

_____

_____

_____

_____

_____

_____

Day _____ **Date** _____

My story for today:

_____

_____

_____

_____

_____

_____

_____

_____

Day _____   **Date** _____

_____

My story for today:

_____

_____

_____

_____

_____

_____

_____

_____

Day _____   **Date** _____

My story for today:

_____

_____

_____

_____

_____

_____

_____

_____

Day _____   **Date** _____

My story for today:

_____

_____

_____

_____

_____

_____

_____

_____

Day _____   **Date** _____

My story for today:

_____

_____

_____

_____

_____

_____

_____

_____

Day _____   **Date** _____

My story for today:

_____

_____

_____

_____

_____

_____

_____

_____

Day _____   **Date** _____

My story for today:

_____

_____

_____

_____

_____

_____

_____

Day _____ **Date** _____

My story for today:

_____

_____

_____

_____

_____

_____

_____

Day _____   **Date** _____

My story for today:

_____

_____

_____

_____

_____

_____

_____

_____

Day _____   **Date** _____

My story for today:

_____

_____

_____

_____

_____

_____

_____

_____

Day _____   **Date** _____

[ ]

My story for today:

_____

_____

_____

_____

_____

_____

_____

_____

Day _____   **Date** _____

My story for today:

_____

_____

_____

_____

_____

_____

_____

_____

Day _____   **Date** _____

My story for today:

_____

_____

_____

_____

_____

_____

_____

Day _____ **Date** _____

My story for today:

_____

_____

_____

_____

_____

_____

_____

_____

Day _____   **Date** _____

My story for today:

_____

_____

_____

_____

_____

_____

_____

_____

Day _____   **Date** _____

My story for today:

_____

_____

_____

_____

_____

_____

_____

_____

Day _____   **Date** _____

My story for today:

_____

_____

_____

_____

_____

_____

_____

_____

Day _____   **Date** _____

My story for today:

_____

_____

_____

_____

_____

_____

_____

_____

Day _____   **Date** _____

My story for today:

_____

_____

_____

_____

_____

_____

_____

_____

Day _____   **Date** _____

My story for today:

_____

_____

_____

_____

_____

_____

_____

_____

Day _____ **Date** _____

My story for today:

_____

_____

_____

_____

_____

_____

_____

_____

Day _____   **Date** _____

My story for today:

_____

_____

_____

_____

_____

_____

_____

_____

Day _____   **Date** _____

My story for today:

_____

_____

_____

_____

_____

_____

_____

Day _____ **Date** _____

My story for today:

_____

_____

_____

_____

_____

_____

_____

Day _____   **Date** _____

My story for today:

_____

_____

_____

_____

_____

_____

_____

_____

Day _____ **Date** _____

My story for today:

_____

_____

_____

_____

_____

_____

_____

_____

Day _____   **Date** _____

My story for today:

_____

_____

_____

_____

_____

_____

_____

_____

Day _____   **Date** _____

My story for today:

_____

_____

_____

_____

_____

_____

_____

_____

Day _____   **Date** _____

My story for today:

_____

_____

_____

_____

_____

_____

_____

_____

Day _____   **Date** _____

My story for today:

_____

_____

_____

_____

_____

_____

_____

Day _____ **Date** _____

My story for today:

_____

_____

_____

_____

_____

_____

_____

Day _____   **Date** _____

My story for today:

_____

_____

_____

_____

_____

_____

_____

_____

Day _____

Date _____

My story for today:

_____

_____

_____

_____

_____

_____

_____

Day _____   **Date** _____

My story for today:

_____

_____

_____

_____

_____

_____

_____

_____

Day _____   **Date** _____

My story for today:

_____

_____

_____

_____

_____

_____

_____

_____

Day _____   **Date** _____

My story for today:

_____

_____

_____

_____

_____

_____

_____

_____

Day _____   **Date** _____

My story for today:

_____

_____

_____

_____

_____

_____

_____

_____

Day _____   **Date** _____

My story for today:

_____

_____

_____

_____

_____

_____

_____

_____

Day _____   **Date** _____

My story for today:

_____

_____

_____

_____

_____

_____

_____

Day _____ **Date** _____

My story for today:

_____

_____

_____

_____

_____

_____

_____

_____

Day _____　　**Date** _____

My story for today:

_____

_____

_____

_____

_____

_____

_____

Day _____   **Date** _____

My story for today:

_____

_____

_____

_____

_____

_____

_____

Day _____   **Date** _____

My story for today:

_____

_____

_____

_____

_____

_____

_____

_____

Made in United States
Orlando, FL
29 August 2022